Space Math

Greg Roza

The Rosen Publishing Group's

READING ROOM
Collection

New York

Published in 2003 by The Rosen Publishing Group, Inc.
29 East 21st Street, New York, NY 10010

Copyright © 2003 by The Rosen Publishing Group, Inc.

First Library Edition 2003

Book Design: Ron A. Churley

Photo Credits: Cover, pp. 1, 14–15, 15 (inset), 20–21, 24 © Digital Vision; pp. 3, 4–5, 7 (left inset), 8 (inset), 10–11, 11 (inset), 12–13, 16 (Earth and Moon insets), 16–17, 19 (all images), 22–23 © PhotoDisc; p. 7 © Jack Zehrt/FPG International; p. 7 (right inset) © Finley-Holiday/FPG International; pp. 8–9 © SuperStock; p. 12 by Ron A. Churley.

Library of Congress Cataloging-in-Publication Data

Roza, Greg.
  Space math / Greg Roza.
    p. cm. — (The Rosen Publishing Group's reading room collection)
Includes index.
Summary: Uses comparisons of the planets in the solar system to practice basic mathematics.
  ISBN 0-8239-3705-4 (library binding)
  1. Mathematics—Juvenile literature. 2. Outer space—Juvenile literature. [1. Mathematics. 2. Outer space.] I. Title. II. Series.
  QA40.5 .R69 2003
  510—dc21
                                    2001008068

Manufactured in the United States of America

For More Information
Outer Space
http://tqjunior.thinkquest.org/5014/

Space-Age Living: Building the International Space Station
http://school.discovery.com/schooladventures/spacestation/

Contents

Earth

Moon

4

What Is Space?

We use the word "space" to name everything there is. The **planet** that we live on—which we call Earth—is very small compared to space. In fact, everything is very small compared to space.

To give you an idea of how big space is, let's take a look at some of the things we can find in it. Our planet is in space. Our Sun is in space. Our entire **solar system** is in space. In fact, space contains so many planets, suns, and solar systems that we cannot count them all!

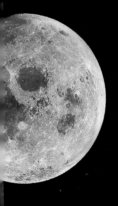

The Moon is the closest object to Earth in space, but it is about 239,000 miles away. If you could drive to the Moon in a car going 50 miles an hour, it would take you about 200 days!

Watching Space

Scientists are discovering new things about space all the time. They do this by studying our solar system, the planets in it, and even space objects that are far away from our solar system. New and powerful tools—like modern **telescopes**—have made studying space easier.

We can learn more about space by comparing our world to other worlds that are millions, **billions**, or even **trillions** of miles away from us. Math is one tool that can help us do this.

The Hubble Space Telescope is the most powerful telescope ever made. It shows us the clearest pictures we've ever seen of stars and galaxies billions of miles away from Earth.

Hubble Space
Telescope

Galaxy

Star Cluster

7

The Speed of Light

Scientists have discovered that light travels at a speed of 186,282 miles a second! We also know that it takes about 8 minutes and 20 seconds—or 500 seconds—for light to travel from the Sun to Earth. We can use these facts to figure out how far it is from Earth to the Sun.

It's not that hard. Multiply the speed of light (186,282 miles a second) by the amount of time it takes sunlight to reach Earth (500 seconds). This equals 93,141,000 miles!

$$\begin{array}{rl} 186{,}282 & \text{miles a second} \\ \times\ \ \ 500 & \text{seconds} \\ \hline 93{,}141{,}000 & \text{miles} \end{array}$$

Do the Math

The closest planet to the Sun is called Mercury. Mercury is 36,000,000 miles from the Sun. How long does it take light from the Sun to reach Mercury? Divide 36,000,000 miles by 500 seconds to find the answer.

A Day in Space

The Earth spins around an **axis**, an imaginary line that runs through Earth from the North Pole to the South Pole. It takes 24 hours, or one day, for Earth to turn all the way around.

It takes Venus—the second planet from the Sun—about 243 Earth days to turn all the way around. If this is true, how can we figure out how many Earth hours there are in a single day on Venus?

If a day on Venus is 243 Earth days long, and an Earth day has 24 hours, all we need to do is multiply 243 days by 24 hours. One day on Venus has a total of 5,832 Earth hours!

Do the Math

If there are 60 minutes in every hour, how many minutes are there in a single day on Venus? Multiply 5,832 hours by 60 minutes to find the answer.

← Axis

Earth

Venus

243 days
x   24 hours
5,832 hours

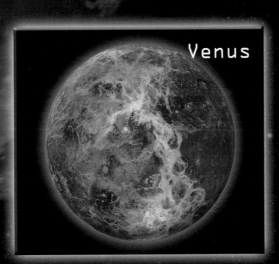

687 days

365 days

Mars

Earth

Sun

687 days
− 365 days
322 days

A Year in Space

It takes about 365 days—or one year—for Earth to travel around the Sun. The farther a planet is from the Sun, the longer it takes to go around the Sun. This means that the planets that are farther away from the Sun than Earth is need more than a year to travel all the way around the Sun.

Mars is the fourth planet from the Sun. It takes Mars about 687 Earth days to go all the way around the Sun. How much longer than Earth does it take for Mars to travel all the way around the Sun?

Subtract the number of days in a year on Earth (365) from the number of days in a year on Mars (687). The answer is 322 days.

Do the Math

How many Earth years does it take for Mars to go around the Sun? To find out, divide the length of a Martian year (687 days) by the length of an Earth year (365 days). Round your answer to the nearest tenth.

Weight in Space

Everything on Earth has weight because of **gravity**, a force that pulls objects toward Earth's center. All planets have gravity. The greater a planet's mass, the greater its gravity. The Sun's gravity is so strong that it holds all the planets in their **orbits**.

Jupiter is the fifth planet from the Sun. The gravity on Jupiter is about 2.5 times stronger than the gravity on Earth. Using this information, how much would a person who weighs 100 pounds on Earth weigh on Jupiter? Multiply 100 pounds by 2.5, and the answer is 250 pounds.

Do the Math

Saturn is the sixth planet from the Sun. The gravity on Saturn is about 1.07 times the gravity on Earth. How much would you weigh on Saturn? Multiply your weight by 1.07 for your answer.

```
  100  pounds on Earth
x   2.5  times the gravity on Earth
  250  pounds on Jupiter
```

Jupiter

Saturn

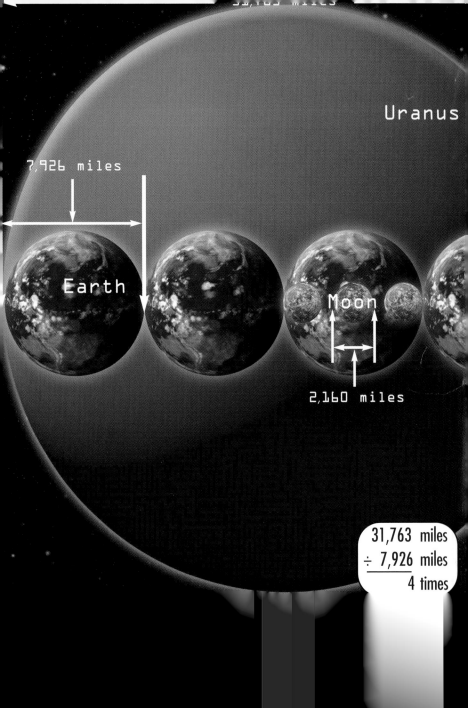

Uranus

7,926 miles

Earth

Moon

2,160 miles

31,763 miles
÷ 7,926 miles
4 times

Planet Size

The **diameter** of Earth from one side to the other straight through its center is 7,926 miles. If you were in a car going 50 miles an hour, it would take about 159 hours to drive that far!

Uranus is the seventh planet from the Sun. The diameter of Uranus is 31,763 miles. How many Earths would you have to put side by side to equal the diameter of Uranus? To find out, divide the diameter of Uranus (31,763 miles) by the diameter of Earth (7,926 miles) and round your answer down to the nearest whole number. The answer is 4.

Do the Math

The diameter of our Moon is 2,160 miles. How many Moons would you have to put side by side to equal the diameter of Earth? Divide 7,926 miles by 2,160 miles, and round your answer down to the nearest whole number.

A Trip Around a Planet

Earth's **circumference** (sir-KUHM-fer-ens) is about 24,900 miles around at the **equator**. If you were in a car traveling on the equator at 50 miles an hour, how many hours would it take you to go all the way around Earth? Divide the length of the equator (24,900 miles) by your speed (50 miles per hour). The answer is 498 hours.

$$\begin{array}{r} 24{,}900 \text{ miles} \\ \div\ \underline{\quad 50} \text{ miles per hour} \\ 498 \text{ hours} \end{array}$$

Neptune is the eighth planet from the Sun. If you could ride in a car traveling around Neptune's equator at 50 miles an hour, it would take you 1,936 hours to circle the planet. If this is true, what is Neptune's circumference at its equator?

$$\begin{array}{r} 1{,}936 \text{ hours} \\ \times\ \underline{\quad 50} \text{ miles per hour} \\ ? \text{ miles} \end{array}$$

Do the Math

Pluto is the ninth planet from the Sun. It would take you about 90 hours to circle Pluto in a car going 50 miles an hour. How far around is Pluto at its equator?

Neptune

equator

Earth

equator

Pluto

equator

19

Comparing Planets

      Study the facts on the table on the opposite page and see if you can answer these questions.

- How long is a day on Jupiter? On Venus?

- Which planet takes the longest amount of time to orbit the Sun? Which takes the shortest amount of time?

- How big is the smallest moon in the solar system? How big is the largest?

- Placed side by side, how many times would the smallest planet in the solar system fit in the largest?

- How far is Uranus from Earth?

- Which planet is not mentioned on this chart?

Do The Math

The biggest moon in the solar system is more than two times bigger than the smallest planet in the solar system!

Fact	Planet	Value
Biggest planet	Jupiter	88,850 miles (diameter at the equator)
Smallest planet	Pluto	1,430 miles (diameter at the equator)
Hottest planet	Venus	864 degrees Fahrenheit
Coldest planet	Pluto	370 degrees Fahrenheit below zero
Longest orbit	Pluto	248 Earth years
Shortest orbit	Mercury	88 Earth days
Longest day	Venus	243 Earth days
Shortest day	Jupiter	10 Earth hours
Most moons	Saturn	18 known moons
Biggest moon	Jupiter (Ganymede)	3,270 miles (diameter at the equator)
Smallest moon	Mars (Deimos)	About 7 miles at widest point
Farthest planet that can be seen without a telescope	Uranus	1,784,000,000 miles from Earth
Believed to be the only planet in the solar system with life on it	Earth	Population in 2002: 6.2 billion people

Scientists have a special way to measure the huge distances of space—the light-year. One light-year equals the number of miles light travels in one year, which is about 5.88 trillion miles!

The closest star to Earth besides the Sun is about 4.4 light-years away! If our Sun were the size of a soccer ball, that star would be about 3,600 miles away, or the number of miles from Alaska to Florida!

Someday scientists hope to visit planets other than our own. Until then, we will need the help of math to learn about worlds billions and trillions of miles away.

> one light year = 5.88 trillion miles
> or 5,880,000,000,000 miles

Glossary

axis   An imaginary line through the center of a planet around which the planet turns.

billion   A large number that means one thousand millions. One billion = 1,000,000,000.

circumference   The distance around a planet.

diameter   The distance from one side of a planet to the other straight through the center.

equator   An imaginary line around the middle of a planet that separates it into two parts, north and south.

gravity   The force that causes objects to move toward the center of Earth and causes planets to circle the Sun.

orbit   A planet's path around the Sun.

planet   A large, round object that moves around the Sun.

solar system   The system made up of our Sun, the nine planets, moons, and other space objects.

telescope   A tool used to make faraway objects look closer and larger.

trillion   A large number that means one thousand billions. One trillion = 1,000,000,000,000.

Index